T0199131

THE ADVENTURES OF
SAM & DAK

A Story of True Friendship

DREW ANNE ALLEN

ILLUSTRATIONS BY REBEKAH COVINGTON

WestBow Press books may be ordered through booksellers or by contacting:

WestBow Press
A Division of Thomas Nelson & Zondervan
1663 Liberty Drive
Bloomington, IN 47403
www.westbowpress.com
844-714-3454

Interior Image Credit: Rebekah Covington

ISBN: 978-1-6642-7502-7 (sc)
ISBN: 978-1-6642-7501-0 (e)

Library of Congress Control Number: 2022914640

Print information available on the last page.

WestBow Press rev. date: 09/01/2022

WESTBOW
PRESS®
A DIVISION OF THOMAS NELSON
& ZONDERVAN

I am Sam, and this is Dak.
I am Deaf, and she is Black.

She likes flowers;

I can't hear, but there's no need,

'cause I can sign,

and she can read.

She's polite, and I am too.
She says please; I say thank you!

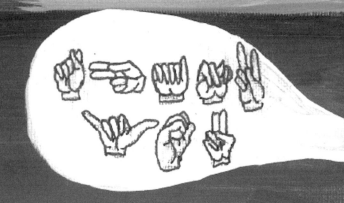

Dak is fun; we play fair.

It works out well when we share.

My mom is Deaf; Dak's is not.

We really like our moms a lot!

She likes math,

and I like art.

Both of us are
really smart!

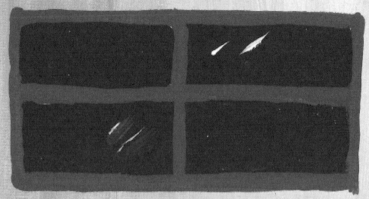

My bike is red;

PROPERTY OF SAM

his wheelchair's blue.

Dak eats sushi; I eat peas.

Sanjay doesn't like either of these!

When we're mad, we work it out,
'cause it's no fun when we just pout!

If I'm sad, she makes me laugh–

then cuts her favorite snack in half.

If someone's mean to my friend Dak,

I stand up and tell them, "Don't do that!"

4G 12:35
GROUP CHAT
YOU'RE UGLY
NO ONE LIKES YOU DAK
SAM
HEY! LEAVE HER ALONG! SHE IS BEAUTIFUL! STOP USING SOCIAL MEDIA TO BULLY HER!
DAK
THANK YOU SAM
NO MORE BULLYING!
BULLY
STOP BEING MEAN!

We like our teacher; she likes us too.

She says we stick together like glue.

Come play with us;
we'll like you too.

There's always room
for someone new!

Deaf or Black, we're all the same.

The only real difference is just your name.

Hey, wait!

We're not done.

Go visit this website, and have more fun!

www.samanddak.com

ABOUT THE AUTHOR:

Drew Anne Allen met a girl named Sam years ago at her very first job at a School for the Deaf. She was earning her master's degree in Deafness at the time, and this led her on to work at the National Technical Institute for the Deaf in Rochester, New York. Later, she worked with Deaf people at the Island Deaf and Hard of Hearing Center on Vancouver Island in beautiful British Columbia. Drew loves the playful feel of rhyme, the value of life lessons learned in everyday life, and, of course, the joys and lessons she's learned from the many Deaf friends she's known along the way.

Printed in the United States
by Baker & Taylor Publisher Services